100 British Limericks
by
James Paterson
ISBN: 978-1-9997156-3-2

Illustrations by Bazmac

Cover photograph of author by Anthony von Roretz

Published by

PUBLISHING

i2i Publishing. Manchester.
www.i2ipublishing.co.uk

Have you heard of the woman from Dover and how her husband wove her? Find out what rhymes with Aberystwyth.

100 British Limericks is a contemporary twist on the traditional limerick form, with a distinctly British feel. By turns whimsical, ridiculous, rude and outrageous, you won't be disappointed. Be careful where you read it though, you might just burst out laughing!

To my mum, for everything

There was a young woman from Dover

Who was covered with hair all over.

On the night that she wed,

In her marital bed,

Her husband just lay there and wove her.

My roof-fixing stint was marred

When I slipped and straddled it hard.

By the pain I was blinded,

I wouldn't have minded

If I hadn't been mending The Shard.

Old Margaret came from near Ely,

Her skin was all flaky and peely.

When asked what she needed,

She finally ceded,

"Well a vacuum cleaner, ideally".

In Maths I'm a total disaster

And in English I need to work faster.

All the kids hate me

And worse still, just lately,

I dislike being headmaster.

When sailing the Solent by boat,

Attached to the mast was a note.

I unfurled it and read it

And gulped as I said it,

"In for repair……DOESN'T FLOAT!"

I once knew a strange physician

Who didn't understand his position.

He used mathematics

To heal asthmatics

And did other odd things in addition.

Fireworks are fun in the Autumn,

But make sure you check where you bought 'em.

My friend bought a rocket

To put in his pocket.

When his balls exploded, I caught 'em.

I picked up my Auntie George

For a closer bond to forge.

I took her to Cheddar

And royally fed her

And watched the fat woman gorge.

There was a young man from Wroot,

His nose was shaped like a flute.

To sneeze was a curse,

When his lips did purse,

From all eight holes it would shoot.

I always feel quite nervous

When standing at the self-service.

There is nothing scarier,

"Check your packing area!"

I now wish a human would serve us.

For my love, I wrote lines of prose.

For her first date, Portsmouth she chose.

It's an odd place to pick for me,

But it turned out a victory.

Later I saw Mary's Rose.

Mike has a fondness for conkers,

They harden in chocolate, it's bonkers.

His strongest beat Sophie's,

He now has eight trophies

And a pantry to match Willy Wonka's.

Where I live, post comes without fail,

Come sun, snow, rain or gale.

The woman at 20

Is giving Pat plenty

And satisfying that Royal Male.

The art of skipping Double-Science

Is feigning your total compliance.

I'm also so smart

To skip double Art

And that is truly a Science.

Last Christmas I put out my stocking

As I heard Santa's sleigh docking.

He quickly got stuck

As he shouted "F**k",

"That's another damn chimney I'm blocking!"

There was an old sergeant named Dance,

He took care of his men in advance.

His subordinate's boil

Filled up with oil.

He suggested the poor corporal lance.

As a teacher, I deal with some urgency

With what is a growing emergency.

The kids' rubbers flinging

And rude in-class singing

Are forming some kind of insurgency.

Old Paddy helps people plant seeds.

He's helpful with gardening needs,

But his awful vision

Explains his decision

To replace the roses for weeds.

There is a young woman from Salisbury.

She strips by my window and calls me,

With a squeaky voice higher

Than the city's great spire.

The sight of her naked appals me.

As I walked on the cliff tops in Whitby,

A visiting foreign count bit me.

It was truly spectacular

That old Mr Dracula

Chose a Sauvignon Blanc to go with me.

Sunday nights are depressing,

Maths homework deadline is pressing.

My laziness peeves me

And in a panicked state, leaves me

Reliant on blind hope and guessing.

When Jenny stormed off on her date,

She left the man screaming, "Wait!"

Her disgust with him started

When he winced and then farted.

She knew what he'd done by his gait.

Keith is recently finding

His teeth are constantly grinding.

He saved all his life

And now his ex-wife

Gets half, which is legally binding.

Nigel's compulsion to lick

Is a most unusual tick.

From what I can gather,

On the windows his slather

Is well over 3 inches thick.

Have you heard of the local baker?

He was an expert bread maker.

He added too much yeast

By ten times at least.

The expanding dough filled an acre.

When Phil swam the Amazon river,

He shuddered and started to quiver.

He let out a screech

As he felt a fat leech

Take a painful route to his liver.

When I play a game of rugby,

A few players in my team bug me.

When I'm in the scrummage,

In my shorts they rummage,

Then try to kiss me and hug me.

There were two boys from Everleigh

Who avoided school quite cleverly.

They skipped double games,

Shimmied down drains

And landed on their balls quite heavily.

While waiting in line for 2 hours,

The mood quite suddenly sours.

Bladder's my nemesis,

Thrown from the premises

And banned from Alton Towers.

There was a young gardener from Epping

Whose plants demanded much prepping.

When I questioned his grumbling,

His answer was humbling,

"It's on my best roses you're stepping".

There was an old man from Fleet

With encrusted cheese on his feet.

Though infected with yeast,

He admitted at least,

It gave him something to eat.

I need social media's assistance

To validate my existence.

Due to my vanity,

I lose my sanity

When my smartphone is kept at a distance.

Sammy is concerned with appearance

And will not tolerate interference.

But when I said all-knowing,

"Your ball bag is showing",

He rushed out to buy cloth adherents.

With skill in defending his wicket,

To the boundary, Tom deftly did lick it.

He never fails

To protect the bails,

But it's football my friend, it's not cricket.

Spiders are supposed to be scary,

But Sammy is smiley and hairy.

He wants to be nice,

Befriends all the mice

And dresses up as a fairy.

In my frenzy to end my last drought,

I drank a whole barrel of stout.

Its condition was squalid

With big lumps of solid.

What it was, I can't figure out.

Danny finds solace in scratching

The spots on his face that are hatching.

His habits cause rumour,

But one point of humour,

His chin has two boils that are matching.

Robin's no whizz kid at chess,

But he's got a head start, I confess.

He has seven kings

And other new things.

His opponent has twelve pieces less.

When playing a rude form of twister

With the seventh and loveliest sister,

I found warts. Where I got em?

One sister's rough bottom.

My skin peeled and started to blister.

There is a young boy from Wrexham,

He pranks his neighbours to vex them.

Parents' phone's ringing,

'Cos eggs he's been flinging.

When they put in new windows, he wrecks them.

The rivers that flow through North Buckingham,

You'd better hope you don't get stuck in them.

Full of discarded brollies

And old shopping trollies,

There's no sign at all of a duck in them.

As the doctor explored every fold

Of Tom's body and wrote down in bold.

"I'll now feel your balls

And how your knob falls".

Tom said, "But I just have a cold!"

There was an old man from Brighton,

He was quite easy to frighten.

Under his bed

Was a man with no head.

Now he sleeps with the light on.

The danger of festival-going

Are the bugs you acquire without knowing.

Even the germs

Are infested with worms

And the toilets are all over-flowing.

There was an old woman from Tealing

Who started to get a strange feeling.

Her neighbour above

Kept declaring his love

Through a little peep hole in the ceiling.

There was a young mother from Merthyr

Who wanted a man that was worth her.

Though fat as a ship,

He allowed her to strip

And found her a dock where he berthed her.

By the time it gets to June,

Englishmen don't think it too soon

To take off their tops,

Out their pasty skin pops.

They burn themselves to a prune.

Mary looks quite bizarre,

She keeps her ear wax in a jar.

When her infection expands,

She uses both hands.

Watch out, she can shoot it quite far.

I wish for a sudden repression

Of our festive shopping obsession.

Stressful buying ensues,

Fellow shoppers enthuse,

While I pray for a massive recession.

Riding escalators in jest

Was something Dan enjoyed best.

His fun turned to terror

When a misjudged error

Saw him dragged deep inside by his vest.

The groundsman at practice at Twickenham,

When balls go wayward through kicking them,

Says, "this'll learn 'em,

Before I return 'em,

I'll make them all slimy by licking 'em."

My girlfriend, I think I might drop 'er,

Her behaviour really 'aint proper.

Her colleagues are loathing

Her absence of clothing

And her use of that cork bottle stopper.

When my car went to the mechanic,

He said that I really should panic.

No amount of tweaking

Could solve the leaking.

It's water tight like the Titanic.

There was a young woman from Imber

Who wished that she was more limber.

Although quite fantastic,

Her limbs were soft plastic

And her torso was chiselled from timber.

I pity poor Malcolm the whale.

At swimming, he always would fail.

He saw a ship,

It gave him a tip,

He used his big fin as a sail.

Belly button ring, navel incision.

Drunk naval mate, lacking precision.

The piercing it seems

Were also my screams,

Of an unwanted slow circumcision.

When visiting the Albert Hall,

I wished I weren't so tall.

For my ticket I fumbled,

Tripped and then tumbled.

From the gods, I took a great fall.

John hasn't washed for a week.

His socks have turned brown and they reek.

His pubes are infested

Where creatures have nested

And his arsehole's developed a beak.

My Dad walked 8 miles to school,

Slept on straw and only ate gruel.

My scolding old gran

Chastised the poor man,

"You were royally pampered, you fool!"

Tony needs glasses for looking,

An optician's visit he's booking.

The wrong type he's picking,

He sweet talks the chicken

And prepares his poor wife for cooking.

There was an old man from Aberystwyth

Whose wife last washed on August 5th.

He urged her to clean,

The stench was obscene.

He used a sponge to scrub her big cyst with.

The problem with my local Balti

Is that all the cookers are faulty.

I ordered a Korma,

It turned out a trauma.

The poppadoms then did assault me.

The trouble with Billy from Burton,

He dances with a very short skirt on.

When a new skirt he gets,

Each person regrets

The lack of a fitting room curtain.

The way to my heart is through feeding,

It ends my undignified pleading.

But the unsightly hummock

That's become of my stomach

Is now prone to internal bleeding.

Kenneth, who lives up in Perth,

Is a gent of significant girth.

When he jumps out his kilt,

Scotland starts to tilt

And shift the axis of the Earth.

There was a young man from Foxham

With a face like a disgruntled oxen.

He was quite a brute,

Fat and hirsuite,

He'd pluck out his pubes and then box them.

Christmas is a time of reflection,

Of Turkey cooked to perfection.

But it would be sweeter

If my friend Peter

Concealed his growing erection.

Hearing bad children scream

Is a common shoppers' theme.

As they purchase fresh dishes,

Each poor mother wishes

Their ordeal was just a bad dream.

There was an old man from Kent

Who caused havoc wherever he went.

He had no mouth

For his breath to come out

And used his arsehole as a vent.

The chicken that crossed the road

Had quite a heavy load.

It's unusual cargo

Was a female called Margo,

A slimy green-horned toad.

The trouble with 'All You Can Eat',

It's come to be seen as a feat

To cram so much food,

That when in the nude,

you can't even see your own feet.

Jeremy went to Pamplona,

But wishes he'd gone with a donor.

Quickly he failed,

As he was impaled.

Now his left testis' a loner.

Last Christmas, with weather all murky,

I decided to do something quirky.

They thought I was bluffing,

I served them burnt stuffing

In a 24-pounder raw turkey.

There was an old man from Reading

Who was excited about his wedding.

He seduced his new bride,

But he couldn't hide

The horrible stains on his bedding.

On ladies' day up in Ascot

I decided to go as a mascot.

When security spied me,

My wife sat astride me.

For a horse I was taken, alas, not.

There was an old man from Crewe

Whose aim always missed the loo.

He sprayed on the seat

And all round his feet.

It wasn't even piss, it was poo.

I'm five and my sister's ten.

That's interesting, that means when

She's a hundred, I'll be fifty

And that's pretty nifty.

I've been learning to double again.

In his pockets, Gerald from Cheltenham

Had something PC Jones felt in 'em.

The policeman's confession,

There was no transgression,

But he enjoyed the time that his hands dwelt in 'em.

The Brits are an unusual breed,

On fish and chips they feed.

Moaning 'bout the weather

Helps them stick together.

A cup of tea's all that they need.

There was a young farmer from Crieff,

His neighbours caused him some grief.

They filled his pants

With spiders and ants

And slithering slugs underneath.

An amorous clown from Bristol

Earns money each night by the fistful.

For his prize circus act,

With 12 friends he's packed

In a phone box. He finds it quite blissful!

One point that I find disgusting,

On my boyfriend's teeth there is crusting.

His gums are receding,

They're puss-filled and bleeding

And his homemade braces are rusting.

Dry January, a new healthy trend

Is good, but was nearly Sam's end.

On day 6, his health failing,

We met. I said wailing,

"You're allowed to drink *water* my friend!!"

There was an old man from Pinner

Who never came home for dinner.

His wife never knew

About his nightly screw

And he ended considerably thinner.

When Pompey gave Saints a good thrashing,

The local supporters kept clashing.

The local constabulary

Caused ripe vocabulary.

Their unrestrained dogs started gnashing.

As Jim's injured back became worse,

He thought he'd been struck with a curse.

With a plan, he lay lurking,

His legs were still working,

One day he ran off with his nurse.

A farmer seen stooped in the rain

Digs nightly amongst his fields' grain.

When each man in Pewsey

Courts his daughter Suzie,

They rest underneath Salisbury plain.

There was a young girl from Dawlish,

Her stature was really quite tallish.

Through an act of contortion,

She skewed each proportion.

Her insides could fit in a small dish.

There was an old woman from Bicester,

She charged men a fiver to kiss her.

This they did rue,

As their lips turned blue,

Swelled and started to blister.

A middle-aged lady from Dorset

Squeezed tightly inside her new corset.

She soon started twitching

As she burst the stitching.

I told her that she mustn't force it.

At a henge of old stones I stood seeing

A huge group of visitors fleeing.

When I questioned a druid,

He mentioned the fluid

I produced when in public I'm peeing.

A fire chief in Central Newham

Had engines but no one to crew 'em.

To douse burning stairways,

He'd ask British airways

To drop water as they overflew 'em.

I always find it unnerving

When my next-door neighbour is perving.

It's hard to ignore

When he waits at my door.

Now a six-year sentence he's serving.

Linda's eyesight is poor,

She's worn glasses since she was four.

In her blinded haste,

She scrubs with toothpaste

To clean the bathroom floor.

I introduce Charlie the camel,

A most magnificent mammal.

With a coat nice and glistening,

Big ears for listening

And his teeth are the brightest enamel.

A pet owner living in Leicester

Disliked those trying to pester.

When they moaned at her habits,

She talked to her rabbits

And their lice that began to infest her.

Our songs at each year's Eurovision

Are the source of a lot of derision.

Norway's not compliant,

On Denmark's reliant

And the basis of Sweden's decision.

A poorly Scotsman gripes

Of a problem of hideous types.

He feels something tilt

Under his kilt,

A twisting of his bag's pipes.

A strange vet living In Birmingham

Enraged dogs and cats by worming them.

She was dogged and catty

and frankly quite scatty.

She mixed them all up when returning them.

I wanted to get rid of Keith, so

I booked him a flight out of Heathrow.

They'd only accept him

If I wrapped him and kept him

Where the suitcases down underneath go.